Words

Words

How to Use
the Power of Words
to Ignite Ideas,
Leverage Connections,
and Influence Others

Tammy Kling

Clovercroft Publishing

Words: How to Use the Power of Words to Ignite Ideas, Leverage Connections, and Influence Others

Published by Clovercroft Publishing, Franklin, Tennessee

Editing by Gail Fallen

Cover Design by Debbie Manning Shepherd

Interior Layout Design by Adept Content Solutions

Printed in the United States of America

978-1-942557-11-1

For my father,
who never could find the right words.

Contents

"Think Big!"

—Jack Ma

Founder and CEO

Alibaba

Words are currency.

They become who you are, ingrained in your heart and soul.

Speak life—to yourself, to your goals, and to your future. Your words can change or save a life. They can (and will) build or destroy relationships. When it comes to the words we speak to ourselves, it's important to understand that your own voice is the most powerful human voice you'll hear as you continue to replay in your subconscious the words that define your reality.

How do you describe yourself?

What words do you use when you look in the mirror?

When you're stressed at work?

Today is the day to replace negative or disempowering words with positive ones. Now is the time to examine the words we use to communicate with ourselves and others.

"Words matter.

Tammy equips

world changers

to change

the world."

—Don Campbell

Founder and CEO

Feeding Children Everywhere

Introduction

How well do you communicate?

Words are an asset or a liability, depending upon how you use them.

We remember the greatest leaders in the world for their words. Their life-changing speeches, inspirational books, and profound quotes live on today, as timeless as the universe itself. Nelson Mandela, Martin Luther King Jr., Lincoln, Jesus, Anne Frank, Winston Churchill, and business and political greats like Buffet, Merkel, and Branson. Words live on as a legacy.

An imprint of your life and your philosophies.

Words can create social influence, another asset that increases your position in relationships, at work with colleagues and management, or with clients. Influence also extends to the way we impact our friends and family. If you cannot influence the ones closest to you, how will you influence the rest of the world? Influence is the ability to get others to see your point of view, and often, act on it. Influence is real and tangible.

You know an influential person when you see them. Even if their words are few, they are good with their words. They know the value of the right words at the right time. Their timing is impeccable. They don't talk over others, but they listen instead. They pause … and speak action-oriented phrases and truths that inspire.

Do you remember the most inspirational words you ever

heard? Maybe it was a teacher, friend, or leader. Maybe a speaker at a motivational conference or a loved one or someone who spoke truth into your life.

When I work with a homeless person on the street or under a bridge, I often find that they have forgotten those positive words. They've clung to the negative ones like a barnacle on the side of a boat. When I sit in the office of a celebrated CEO and listen to him weep about his childhood as he shares his story, those old words that wounded him are revealed once again. Words matter. The good ones lift and elevate, inspiring

Words matter. The good ones **lift** and **elevate,** inspiring cultures and families and teams to **greatness.**

cultures and families and teams to greatness. The bad ones stay with us until we decide to let them go.

Investing in words is the biggest investment you can make. They add value to your life and business and strengthen your relationships. Better words make you better. They will alter your identity and empower you to new heights, changing you from the inside out.

Investing in Words is the biggest investment you can make.

Most of us don't think much about the words we use because we've been speaking since childhood. Talking is a basic skill, and we do not generally focus on the way we use words or how well we use them as we progress through life. At times you may

have attended a speakers class
or presentation course that was
focused on delivering a talk. But
the words we are focusing on in
this book are the daily words we
speak silently to ourselves and
the words we speak out loud
to others.

**This is a book to help you use
more powerful words.**

8 Simple Truths

about

Words

that will change

the way you

see the world

Think

"Stand on what is true and do not let go."

—John Elderedge

Author

Wild at Heart

Words are currency

There is no greater wealth than the wealth inside you.

Whether you are rich or poor, you have the exact same resources as the person sitting beside you.

We are all born as infants with a body and a brain and flailing arms and the ability to make sounds. The same. When we begin to form words, we soon learn that some words gain us specific rewards like a ball or a bottle or a cookie.

A mother shrieks with delight at a child's first word, and from the very first moment we make the connection between the word and the reward, we learn this truth:

I can get things with words. Words are currency. But then, as life goes by, and we continue along the path of life day in and day out speaking words upon words upon words, we forget just how valuable those words really are. We view words merely as a method of communication. "I'd like the New York Strip," we tell the waitress, and we receive it. It's just the way the world works.

Start being intentional about your words. Because here's the truth:

words
are currency.

In fact, we can often become complacent with our words. We begin to take on the words of the people around us until we hardly notice what we're saying. But now is the time to reverse that and start being intentional about your words. Because here's the truth: words are currency.

A corporation can lose millions of dollars with just one employee using the wrong words in the wrong way face-to-face with a client or on social media.

Justine Sacco was a PR executive who destroyed her career with just one racist tweet. She sent the tweet before boarding a flight to Africa, and by the time she landed, it had created a shocking Buzz that went viral. Justine was fired for one random sentence. Here's a woman who has built a career on words. As a PR expert, it was her job to sell clients and develop their PR campaigns, yet she was careless with her own words.

News outlets wrote about Justine for days and then weeks, and she became a poster child for what went wrong when corporate America didn't address

the danger of unintentional communication.
How do we respond in social media on our personal accounts? How does that reflect in our careers? You may think it doesn't matter, but in a transparent society where everyone sees everything, it does. Remember that everyone's watching.
Even your best customer and your aunt, future boss, or your mother.

Every photo and word we post is open for the world to see.

Organizations and individuals need to be mindful about educating and training employees to be aware of what they say.

A friend of mine saw a nurse wearing a bikini on Facebook, and in the photo, the nurse was drinking a big gigantic beer on a party boat. Her other photos

were the same. In every photo
she looked intoxicated, although
she was certainly having fun.
Her words on the post were a
combination
of obscenities
and random
rantings. When
my friend had
an injured
child, she
deliberately
drove to a
hospital a bit
further away
to avoid that
ER nurse—the woman in charge
at the hospital closest to her.
It wasn't that she thought the
nurse was a bad person. But her
party-animal photos created a
lack of credibility and lost the
hospital a customer.

Remember that everyone's watching. Even your best customer and your aunt, future boss, or your mother.

Some people will think that's
harsh. But it is your right to
determine how you feel about
what someone says and how they

act, and we do it each and every day.

That's your ability to make a judgment. When you make a judgment, you judge for yourself what is right for you and your family and your business. You have that right. Judgment is a positive act, because otherwise, you'd be moving through life blindly without thinking. So when it came time to make a choice, the question in the mother's mind was simple. Do I want the party-girl nurse handling my most important asset? The answer was no.

Words can cost you money or make you money.

Think back to your first real job interview and how you walked out of that face-to-face meeting either confident or insecure. I remember mine well. It was a

series of stressful interviews.
I had to use and choose words
wisely. I remember the thrill of
adrenaline and the nervousness
and the loud beat of my heart
as I answered a firing squad of
questions. Words are currency.

BE INTENTIONAL with your words.

That includes colleagues, clients, and everyone in your life.

Make a list of the five most powerful words you can think of:

1

2

3

4

5

Change

"Words are weapons."

Words change lives

What if we were more intentional about the words we used?

Words can breathe life or death into a situation.

The words you use in writing, whether in a text, email, or in a book, can change and even save a life.

Do you remember the words that impacted your life the most?

Mine are "your father committed suicide." Those four words changed the trajectory of my life forever. They are the words that created a crater in my heart yet infused it with purpose all at once.

When I was asked to give a TEDx talk, it wasn't difficult to find the topic. Words save lives. Words are currency. Use your words today.

I always wondered how life would have been different for my father if he had met someone like me on that last day, someone who would have intercepted his negative self-talk and given him the right words to fuel hope in his life. Would he have made a different decision?

The words you use in writing, **whether in a** text, email, or book, **can change and even save a life.**

You cannot change someone's action, and you aren't responsible for it. We all make our own decisions. But you can interrupt a bad plan by speaking life into someone else's life. By stopping for a moment on the side of the road to ask a stranger what's wrong. By reaching out to a child, an abused wife, or a man who might need a hand up. Someone may need your word. The word that is inside you, the one you know that it's time for you to deliver. You may be the messenger that is uniquely suited to deliver that one message to someone who might be moved, and then changed forever, by your words.

What if the one in need is a coworker?

People in various positions of influence all over the world struggle with hopelessness, depression, and anxiety. Oftentimes their negative self-talk is so strong by the time they've reached that point that they're focusing on their failures instead of their successes.

But I've found that one conversation can catapult a life to a different level. I've seen the most hopeless human transform after I've given them hope.

Anyone can do it. It just takes a commitment to using words that change lives.

Bus driver Darnell Barton saw a woman about to jump from an overpass. He stopped his bus on a busy highway with a busload of passengers to talk to her. He reached his arm around the despondent woman and pulled her to safety. One quick conversation coupled with swift action saved that woman's life.

Reach out to those around you, and be aware of when someone is in need. You might be surprised how well your words are received when you're in the right place at the right time.

"You were

the only one

who saw me."

—Nate Houston

homeless

Inspire

Relationships are built on conversations

Every relationship we build will impact our business life or life in general. Whether it's a relationship with the colleague in the next cubicle or corner office, or your kids soccer coach or teacher, that relationship can impact the way you feel.

If you think about your deepest relationships, they have been built by a series of conversations. We talk, connect, and our interaction makes sense. I get you, and you get me. We want to talk more, and it is a series of conversations—via text, by phone, or face-to-face—that connect us.

Relationships are everything, and when we feel as if someone isn't listening or as if they do not respect what we say, the conversation deteriorates. The relationship suffers or is weakened.

When I worked in corporate sales management for American Airlines, I created something called the customer salesforce.

The idea emerged from my excellent relationships with customers. I had always taken a casual conversational approach to selling because I really didn't feel as if I was the sales type at all. I used words to generate excitement about our service and to talk intelligently with CEOs and corporate executives.

It was my role to increase market share within my client companies at high management levels, and I worked with companies like Burger King and Schlumberger as well as

Dell and many other major companies. I found myself connecting personally with many of these customers and just simply developing excellent relationships. One of my customers was a major influencer at a prospect I was trying to present to, and I invited my customer from one company to go with me to my initial sales presentation at another company! The outcome was a beautiful process of credibility building through a customer salesforce.

We talk, connect, and our interaction makes sense. **I get you, and you get me.** We want to talk more.

My customer already had a relationship with my prospect, so my customer ended up doing all the selling for me. The conversations had already taken place, and the result was a series of connected relationships. Leverage the power of words to create a network of authentic service-minded people who want to see you grow. Don't underestimate the power of a conversation.

Some of the greatest thought leaders and teachers in the world are great conversationalists. The art of conversation is just that, the ability to artistically and beautifully weave words together. It is the act of listening—and then answering—thoughtfully.

Become a master at the art of conversation.

Don't use can't

Use the word "you" to captivate your audience

What words do you use in presentations at work, or special documents, papers, or marketing materials? How about in email? Conversation styles become as apparent as clothing styles after you interact with someone and see their pattern. Some people are used to writing short, curt responses, while others write long, very formal, answers to a simple email.

No matter what the medium, the words we use to communicate the message should be directed toward the audience—and away from you.

What exactly does this mean? Use the word "you" in order

to engage the heart, talk with influence, and get results. If you use the word "I" or ignore the reader altogether and just vomit out your words and statistics and facts to make a point, you might be damaging your desired outcome.

The words we use to communicate the message **should be** **directed toward the audience**—and away from you.

In business negotiations, listening for what the person on the other side wants is key. Then you can craft your response and the right words around it.

Nearly every book I've ever edited or helped create bore the mistake of being too self-centric on the author. When we're crafting a bestseller, I coach authors to be mindful of the audience and his or her desire to know more about themselves. Great philosophers like Aristotle

and Plato are still revered today
because man is still in search of
himself. So he searches through
the halls of libraries, reading
books about philosophy and
religion and a myriad of other
things in search of the answers.
The self-help industry alone
churns out millions of books read
by millions of people worldwide.

This one secret is most often
overlooked, and I have yet to
see many writers utilize it. It's
human nature to write or talk
about the facts or the story
you're trying to communicate.
It's not human nature to start by
ignoring all of that and focusing
on the reader.

I have a very specific formula
that I take a reader through
when I'm writing a book. That's
the addition of questions to
engage the reader's heart. Why?
Because the audience wants to
connect with you and hear you,

and they will do both if you talk about them and their issues. If you can solve their issue, even better.

Use the power of you. Engage the reader. If it's a speech, onstage, or if you're an executive addressing employees, do the same thing. In a book or a talk, here's how it looks:

Example:

"For the past decade I've been onstage speaking to audiences in thirty-four countries across the globe about healthcare."

Not a bad sentence, right?

What if we tweaked it just slightly?

"What does being healthy mean to you?
"For the past decade I've been onstage speaking to audiences in

thirty-four countries across the globe about healthcare."

See the difference? In the second option, the person talking has instantly engaged the reader. By asking a question, you show the reader or audience member that you care and that you're about to deliver something important.

They listen—because you've asked a question that applies to their life.

The audience wants to connect with you and hear you, and they will do both if you talk about them and their issues.

I write books about such topics as healthcare, business, leadership, transformation, and culture. Words are a corporate leader's way of communicating ideals to clients. And how about internal communication—words meant to educate, unite, and inspire employees?

Corporate communications is one of the biggest assets within a business.

I'm in the right business for the next decade. Words don't go out of style.

Be powerfully intentional about your words.

Do so not only in business but also in your personal life, on Facebook and Twitter, and with your loved ones, your children and your friends.

What words do you use?

You

We are all motivational speakers

In corporate America, the biggest bonding tool among teams is the spoken word. Great leaders inspire and empower. People want to follow them. Mediocre leaders don't.

When you think about the words you use each and every day, think of their impact. Why not consider yourself a mentor?

Walk into the office and decide that you will intentionally talk positively to a stranger, a colleague, and everyone you meet. Don't let one negative word exit your mouth. When you're faced with an obstacle or adversity, hold your tongue and let it pass. Start to use your words like dollars. If you had only twenty to spend an hour, you'd be more careful with them. Think of yourself as a motivational speaker, and think of your words as an asset. Invest in the right ones.

How do you talk to your own family?

What words do you use at work with colleagues or clients?

How about on social media?

If you don't use your words wisely, they will be used as a weapon against you.

One of the observations I've made in my decade working with corporations is that they don't train employees on the word aspect of social media. Training is focused on compliance, or employees in some organizations are banned from using social media at work. But they're not being trained to consistently use the right words in their own private lives on their social media accounts. It's not about monitoring your every move or censorship. It's about teaching people why words matter, how to create a values-based message.

Why not consider yourself a mentor?

In today's world everyone with a business is focused on social media. Unfortunately, the effort to meet online requirements for SEO (search engine optimization) in order to get their brand and name out there often results in some pretty mediocre content.

That's not good for any individual or organization. It's not just how visible you are that matters. It's what you say and how you say it. Is your message authentic? Do your words resonate clearly with the heart of the person you're speaking to? When you go to make a presentation to a client, do they relate to and understand what you say?

What are the words that you remember most?

The words you use cement your legacy.

Words are the foundation for building businesses, teams, and relationships.

Power

The right words build cultures, businesses, and brands

Words tell the story of a business, and smart companies know it.

Those who brand themselves by appealing to the deepest desires of the human spirit make the biggest impact on the world. One of my book clients is the CEO of Feeding Children Everywhere, an organization that feeds hungry kids all over the world. It's not hard to tell the story of that organization, because they're in the business of saving lives. But for other businesses, we've got to dig deeper to communicate the real message behind the story in a way that matters.

That's my expertise. Finding the meaning for the audience and the words to build the bridge and ignite change.

Companies that inspire and encourage are the winners in today's market. Here's an example of how it works.

Scroll through any of these Reebok Spartan Race ads, and you can't help but be inspired! They make me want to go outside and run around in the mud like a warrior even when I'm scrolling through emails, still in my pajamas.

So in an instant, with an image and a message, Reebok has captured my attention. Why? Because instead of picturing a shoe or a product, they're delivering a story and a promise. Strong companies and messages deliver a promise.

The promise cannot be hollow. It has to be deep, even primal, as it reminds us to reach for something better. Join the race, get off the couch, leave your hurts and fears behind. There's a warrior inside you. Tap into it.

This is the message Reebok sends through their word and visual campaign about the Spartan race. Some of your message will appeal to the audience on a subconscious level.

We've got to dig **deeper** to communicate the **real message** behind the story in a way that **matters.**

Writing and communicating the right message must involve appealing to the six senses. Every step of the way, we are listening, activating, breathing in, and watching. Today's consumer breathes, reads, clicks, double clicks, deletes, hits send, and replies all at once within a ten-second sound bite. Messages must be crisp, concise, and yet measured with depth. Don't be too shallow and don't be too contrived.

This is what I do. Create the promise and deliver that to the audience. Because anyone can make a shoe. But not just anyone can give you adventure. And adventure is what we all want more of.

Today, it's the storytellers that win.

It's about inspiring people to see that they can do anything, be anything, and achieve much more than they ever envisioned before.

What are the words that will best encapsulate and sell your business? What product or book do you want to market? The old days of providing just a good product are over.

Starbucks proved that a long time ago.

It's about the experience and the story.

Today, it's the storytellers that win.

I spend a lot of my time refining business messages that will set organizations apart. A message and a story that will catapult them to the top of their industry.

If you have a company, you had better also have an authentic amazing story to go along with it. Today the consumer wants reality and authenticity. Be as real as you want. The author of Harry Potter did, making sure that she told her story about being a poor single mom and writing her book. It was a story that people liked and related to. It was a story that had struggle. Apple encouraged us to think differently. Isn't it refreshing?

When I go into an organization and talk about how to use words to build influence and relationships with prospective clients—and internally amongst teams—it's about these three things.

Be real (now more than ever) Appeal to people's desire for adventure and freedom, and it will set you apart.

Use vibrant images and words that are congruent.

Use shorter sentences to create velocity.

Today's consumer expects authenticity, and that's great news for all of us. Be you.

Sticks
and stones
can break
my bones,
but
words
will never
hurt me

Your story matters

Don't ever underestimate the power of your life story. No matter what challenges you've faced at work or at home, your story matters. It is as relevant as the CEO or the professional NFL player or celebrity. Your life struggle is the fuel that can change someone else's. Share your story.

When I was interviewed for the Discovery Channel, the producer asked me if I was simply attempting to rewrite the story by writing all these books in an attempt to save lives. My Italian publisher asked me the same thing. I suppose at the soul level, that's true. Aren't we all driven by that shard of glass in our soul? And if not, shouldn't we be? We are driven by our victories and losses. Most of the people who come to me to write a book have achieved great things, but it hasn't been without some adversity along the way.

NFL player Al Smith described a series of football victories until the one day we had a call and I asked him: "What was the worst moment of your life?"

Al described a game, in which he had just come off the field, like any other game and when he was undressing in the locker room, a coach came by and summoned him. "You need to get to first aid," the coach said. Al described to me the anxiety that began to build as he quickened his pace. He began the long walk to first aid, and when he got there, he saw people crying. His fiancée had

Your life struggle is the fuel that can change someone else's.

choked on a piece of food and died. Right there in the stands. Watching his game.

As we replayed that story again, I realized the gravity of it. I've sat with many grown men who had achieved great things and listened to their stories. Many times, those stories are tragic, and that tragedy brings back memories. Al described how devastating his experience had been. But as the years passed, he developed a love for life and an appreciation for it like never before. It was an indelible understanding of how important every moment is.

Your words have power.

Throughout the course of history, words have built nations, started and ended wars, solidified relationships, and created incredible life-changing films and books.

TED is a platform built on the power of words. Because we all have ideas, but words bridge the gap between worlds. You cannot spread ideas without words.

The best words I receive today come in the form of love letters from my boys, Reed and Luke. It is the simplest most beautiful form of love.

Use your words today.

Courage

Influence is an asset

What's your influence IQ?
Your influence is determined
by the impact or results of your
words.

Influence is one of the single
most important business and
life assets.

How much influence you have
can be easily assessed by
analyzing your connecting points
and speed of results.

Can you call people and connect
them to others at a moment's
notice? Are you connected
with world changers? Can you
get things done when your
management asks you to or
when you need something? An
influencer has already built

equity through a series of conversations. It doesn't happen overnight. It's an investment in others and a genuine desire to give more than you receive.

One of my clients has a philosophy to "give more than is expected."

This theory has won over the hearts of so many people he has served and given to throughout the years that he has built a large and influential business and personal social network. It's his philosophy to "do favors in advance," and he does. I'll never forget him telling me how Zig Ziglar was an early mentor of his who modeled using words to encourage others and actions to let them know you care. He brought me to Zig's eightieth birthday party, and we watched Zig onstage not talking about himself, but about the others who had impacted his life. When you give more than is expected, you create a lasting impression.

One day a truck drove up and a man began installing something really large in my back yard. It looked like a replica of the Ritz Carlton ... on a pole. But it was a birdhouse! This amazingly handcrafted structure was installed on a twenty-five-foot pole outside my bedroom window.

An influencer has already built equity through a series of conversations.

I hadn't done anything to deserve it, but it was given in appreciation for the work my client and I had done together on a book. His motto to "do favors in advance" wasn't a bunch of words strung together. He actually did it. When your words line up with your actions, people start to believe in you.

You build influence, and it grows.

When you have influence, you can pick up the phone—call leaders of companies, nations, or communities—and make things happen. When you have influence, people write about you, talk about you, and include you in their plans for the future. Influence is magnetic and it transforms lives and businesses.

Authentic influence is **powerful** and **productive**.

Leverage your influence. Work to build relationships and increase your influence IQ this year. Authentic influence is powerful and productive. Entrepreneurs need influence for growth, expansion, credit, connections, and results. Leaders within an organization need influence to get things done.

After years of investing and building trust equity, you find that people respond quickly when you request something. One call gets results.

World changers are action-oriented influencers. They make plans, execute easily, and pull together others who will drive change.

The currency we all work for (money) allows us to buy products and services across the globe. We work for money, save it, spend it, gift it, and work for more. But there's no currency more powerful than influence. Influence can be used on every continent. Make no mistake—an influential woman or man has power that can change the decisions of world leaders, executives, businesses, and families.

Over the years I began noticing that I had built a level of

influence money can't buy. My mission was to change lives through the written word, and the books I wrote made a lasting impact. At times I partnered with CEOs and celebrities and nonprofits on books. I remained open to new partnerships, and my network exploded.

I became a connector who invested in others naturally. I did a lot for other influencers for free simply because I wanted to see them shine.

And this is the cornerstone of influence. Influencers have a sense of community and confident strength. They hang around with other influencers, and like iron sharpens iron, they grow through the power of multiplication.

What ideas can you ignite with your influence today? How can you sharpen your words and ideas to become more authentically influential?

"Work smart.

Get things done."

—Susan Wojcicki

CEO

YouTube

Your words **MATTER.**

What's your story?

General Notes

Words matter. What you say is as important as how often and where you say it. It's not about social media. It's about social influence.

Need help with words?
If you need a communications expert to refine your message or help write your legacy or corporate book, contact Tammy.
www.tammykling.com

Tammy Kling is a global bestselling author who uses words to change lives. As the CEO of OnFire Books, Tammy helps leaders of companies and humanitarian organizations, create content that tells their story.

Tammy has written 175 books with professional athletes, entrepreneurs, extraordinary humans, and CEOs. In the healthcare industry her book *Optimal Health*, was a recent New York Times list bestseller. Tammy has books in several countries and languages including the book *The Compass*.

She's been featured on the Discovery Channel, Oprah radio, Huffington Post, and *Dateline NBC* among others. Virgin. com called Tammy one of the world's top ghostwriters. Tammy's TEDx talk is Words are Currency.

Tammy speaks all over the world about the power of words.

Printed in the USA
CPSIA information can be obtained
at www.ICGtesting.com
JSHW012042140824
68134JS00033B/3206

9 781942 557111